A FIREFLY BOOK

Published by Firefly Books Ltd. 2014

First printing

Publisher Cataloging-in-Publication Data (U.S.)

De la Bédoyère, Camilla.
Creatures of the night / Camilla de la Bédoyère.
[80] pages : col. ill., col. photos. ; cm.
Includes index.
Summary: A collection of animals who are active at night. Drawings and photographs highlight how each animal hunts, sees and moves by night.
ISBN-13: 978-1-77085-459-8 (pbk.)
1. Nocturnal animals – Behavior – Juvenile literature. I. Title.
591.5 dc 23 QL755.5D343 2014

Library and Archives Canada Cataloguing in Publication

De la Bédoyère, Camilla, author
Creatures of the night / Camilla de la Bédoyère.
Includes index.
ISBN 978-1-77085-459-8 (flexibound)
1. Nocturnal animals—Juvenile literature. I. Title.
QL755.5.D43 2014   j591.5'18   C2014-901597-6

Published in the United States by
Firefly Books (U.S.) Inc.
P.O. Box 1338, Ellicott Station
Buffalo, New York 14205

Published in Canada by
Firefly Books Ltd.
50 Staples Avenue, Unit 1
Richmond Hill, Ontario L4B 0A7

Printed in China by 1010 International Ltd

Conceived, designed, and produced by
Marshall Editions
A division of the Quarto Group
The Old Brewery, 6 Blundell Street
London, N7 9BH UK

Editors: Emma Marriot and Jon Richards
Designers: Malcolm Parchment,
Marissa Renzullo, and Siân Willams
Art Director: Susi Martin
Publisher: Zeta Jones

CREATURES OF THE
NIGHT

CAMILLA DE LA BÉDOYÈRE

FIREFLY BOOKS

CONTENTS

LIVING IN THE DARK

Many animals battle to survive in the shadowy world of the night. Blanketed by darkness, most nocturnal animals have special adaptations, such as super senses, that help them to find food, attract a mate, or stay safe from predators.

SENSING SOUND

Nocturnal animals have a good sense of hearing. They can listen out for the sounds of movements. Snakes have almost lost their sense of hearing. Instead, they "hear" by sensing vibrations that travel through their bones.

SIGHT AT NIGHT

Bushbabies have huge eyes with a special layer inside called the tapetum lucidum, which reflects light. Other nocturnal animals, such as cats, also have light-reflecting eyes.

Bushbabies need good eyesight to hunt bugs at night.

Coiling tail
Tree-dwelling pit vipers coil their tails around branches to hold on tight while they lie in wait to ambush prey.

Heat detectors
Two heat-sensitive pits are located between the eyes and nostrils.

Scales
The scales of this snake are yellow, but many other pit vipers are green, brown, or even pinkish in color.

Flickering tongue
Snakes constantly flick out their tongues to pick up smells in the air around them.

A cricket chirps by rubbing its wings together.

NIGHT NOISES

Most of the time, nocturnal animals keep quiet to avoid the attention of predators. Sometimes, they need to make a loud noise to attract a mate, or to warn love rivals to stay away.

A kiwi's nostrils are on the tip of its sensitive beak.

DARK SMELLS

Kiwis are nocturnal animals from New Zealand. Their eyesight is poor but they have the best sense of smell of any bird, and can sniff out prey using their beaks. As they walk they tap the ground with their long beaks to disturb worms and bugs.

Silent slitherer
The long body of a snake is the perfect shape for slithering along the ground—or branches— and striking at prey in total silence.

Hooded eyes
The eyelash viper has curious scales above the eyes that look like eyelashes. These help break up the snake's outline when it is hiding in foliage.

⊕ FEELING THE HEAT

The pit viper can feel the heat of prey and predators nearby. Using the heat-sensitive pits on its head, it not only senses an animal's presence, but also judges its distance and the direction in which it is moving. Then the snake strikes, sinking poisonous fangs into its victim.

GRAY WOLF

Gray or timber wolves are the largest wild members of the dog family. They are found in the northern hemisphere, in North America, Europe, and Asia. Wolves live in family groups called packs. Each pack is led by two "top dogs"—a male and female pair.

WHAT TO EAT

Wolves are carnivores (meat-eaters). They mostly feed on large animals, such as elk, bison, and moose. But lone wolves eat smaller prey such as beavers, rabbits, and even mice.

Going fishing
In some places, hungry wolves find that a fish makes a good meal.

HOWLING

Wolves howl to call for mates, to tell wolves from other packs to stay away, or to communicate with other members of their own pack. Howling can go on for hours at a time.

A wolf's howl can be heard up to 6 miles (10 km) away.

Fur
Thick, shaggy fur covers the wolf's body, keeping it warm through long, cold winters.

SIZE • 3¼–5 FT

0   5 ft

⊕ WILD PETS

All of the world's pet dogs are descended from gray wolves. These nocturnal hunters once roamed over large parts of the world. Today, they keep away from humans and mostly live in forests or mountains.

Ears
Wolves can move their ears to pick up sounds coming from any direction.

Wolf packs vary in size and can have between two and 15 members.

Muzzle
Members of the dog family have a long snout, called a muzzle. It is packed with smell-sensitive cells.

PACK OF WOLVES

Wolves travel, sleep, eat, and hunt together. The members of a pack are related to each other. Only the top dogs—a male and female pair—have cubs.

⊕ ON THE HUNT

Wolves rely on their sense of smell to find their prey, which they track together. By working as a group, the pack can follow and catch large animals such as caribou (a type of deer). The top dogs feed first, and the other members of the pack must wait until they have finished before being allowed to eat.

FACT FILE

DIET
Most large mammals

HABITAT
Woodland, forests, and grasslands

WOLVES AND DOGS

Members of the dog family are called canids. Like many other carnivores, canids often hunt at night, when they can rely on their incredible sense of smell to find prey. Canids are powerful animals that run long distances to pursue their prey. This animal group includes dogs, wolves, coyotes, jackals, and foxes.

The fur is thick and reddish-brown.

Long legs
Maned wolves have long legs and bushy tails, like most other canids. Their long legs may help them to peer above tall grass.

ASIAN WILD DOG
The dhole, or Asian wild dog, has a dark tail and quite short legs. These canids live and hunt in groups, and a pack shares the care of the pups. Unlike most members of the wild dog family, dholes wag their tails.

MANED WOLF
Maned wolves are intelligent, curious animals. They spend most of the day resting under plants where they can stay cool in the hot sun of the South American grasslands. They come out to hunt as the sun goes down.

⊕ LONE HUNTERS

Unlike gray wolves, maned wolves live alone or as a pair. They stay within their own home areas, called territories, and fight other maned wolves that come too close. These meat-eaters also eat insects, fruit, and roots.

A jackal hopes to scare other animals away by standing tall and baring its teeth.

JACKAL

There are at least three different types of jackal. They are found across Africa, and can survive in deserts where they hunt small mammals, birds, lizards, and snakes. Jackals live as pairs, or in packs.

Looking bigger
The dark hair on the back of the neck can stand on end, giving the appearance of a mane and making the wolf look bigger.

Pouncing hunters
Canids chase their prey but maned wolves and coyotes also pounce on small animals, and deliver a deadly bite.

AFRICAN WILD DOG

A pack of African wild dogs can hunt large animals including zebra and antelopes. These canids are fearless predators that are not afraid to hunt in the full light of day. However, when the moon is full, they become nocturnal.

Wild dogs are also known as "painted dogs" because of their fur's strange coloring.

FENNEC FOX

Fennec foxes are not only the smallest members of the fox family, they are also the smallest of all canids. They live in the Sahara Desert—one of the world's hottest places, where daytime temperatures can top 120°F (50°C). Many desert animals are nocturnal, and sleep throughout the scorching day.

BURROW HOMES

Fennec foxes dig burrows where they can rest and stay out of the burning African sun. They also use their dens to rear their young, which are called pups or cubs.

Fennec foxes stay in their dens until sunset.

HUGE EARS

These little foxes have huge ears and an incredible sense of hearing. They find most of their food by listening to the sounds of animals moving underground. They can even hear beetles burrowing. Once a fox has heard its prey, it digs through the sand to find it.

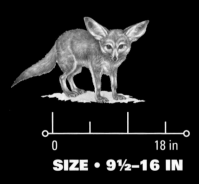

0   18 in

SIZE • 9½–16 IN

PUPS

Pups are born blind and helpless. Their eyes open when they are two weeks old, and just a few weeks later, the pups can play together.

At five weeks of age, pups begin to explore outside the den.

Big ears
The fox's ears measure 4–6 inches (10–15 cm) long. Its body is smaller than that that of a pet cat.

Night vision
The eyes have a special layer (the tapetum) that reflects light and helps the fox to see in the dark.

Sand-colored fur
helps to camouflage the fox.

DESERT DIET

Fennec foxes eat anything from fruit and seeds to eggs and small animals. To catch speedy animals such as lizards and insects, they need both stealth and fast reactions.

⊕ LIFE IN THE DESERT

These foxes are suited to life in the desert. They can survive for days without a drink of water. Like an elephant, a fox's ears also help it to keep cool. Large ears lose heat more quickly than small ears.

Heat protection
The fox's paws—including the soles—are covered with fluffy fur that helps to protect the animal's skin from the hot desert sand.

FOXES

Foxes are members of the dog family, but they usually have snouts that are longer and more slender than those of their dog cousins. Most foxes are also smaller than other canids and have very bushy tails. They live in almost all parts of the world, but they are shy animals that prefer to avoid humans.

These predators *sometimes hunt in the day if there are no humans around.*

PAMPAS FOX

"Pampas" is the South American word for grassland. Pampas foxes spend the day hiding in dens that may be decorated with found objects, such as bits of cloth.

RED FOX

Of all foxes, the red fox is the most successful. This animal is very adaptable. It can hunt in both the day and night, and will eat almost anything.

Fur color can be anything from orange-red to deep brown, gray, or even black.

WINTER CAMOUFLAGE

In winter, Arctic foxes grow white fur that is camouflaged against the snow, so they blend into their habitat. They hunt small, furry animals called lemmings, but they will also eat almost anything they can find, including dead animals.

COLD SURVIVAL

Life in the Arctic is hard. The fox's paws are covered in fur, and extra blood flows into them, so they don't freeze on the ice. Cubs are born in the summer, when there is more food, and both parents look after them.

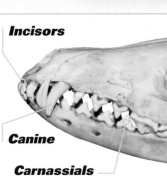

Incisors

Canine

Carnassials

Molars

FOX SKULL

Foxes and other canids have teeth that are suited for a variety of foods. Incisors at the front are general biting teeth. Fangs, or canine teeth, work like daggers to stab prey, and molars crush bones and plants. The side teeth—carnassials— work like scissors to cut flesh.

Stay small
This fox has short legs, and its head and ears are small. This helps the animal to keep its body heat.

White coats
During winter, an Arctic fox's hairs are long, and packed tightly together to trap warm air against the fox's skin. A number of Arctic foxes have darker, gray-bluish coats.

After the winter, *the Arctic fox grows a new coat of shorter, brownish fur that blends in with the summer plants.*

HONEY BADGER

Honey badgers have powerful bodies and huge claws, which they use to dig. They hunt animals to eat, but they are most famous for their love of bees and honey. These predators belong to a group of animals known as mustelids.

Shoulders
The shoulders and chest are broad and packed with muscles.

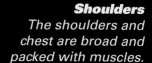

HONEY BADGER SKULL

A honey badger's head is small for the size of its body, but the jaw is still capable of a powerful bite.

Huge canines grab prey

Slicing teeth cut meat

Like canids, *mustelids have different teeth to perform different jobs.*

0   36 in

SIZE • 23–30 IN

Digging feet
The front feet are used for digging. They are bigger than the hind feet, and have larger claws.

⊕ ON THE DEFENSE

Honey badgers use their huge teeth and claws to scare away big animals, such as lions. They also have a natural resistance to snake venom—if bitten, they may go into a coma but will then recover. This means they can kill and eat even large, venomous snakes such as cobras.

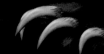

Hives are full of honeycomb, which is dripping with honey.

Thick fur
The fur is dark and dense. The mantle is a broad gray-white stripe that runs from the head to the tail.

TASTY TREAT

Honey badgers use their superb sense of smell to find beehives. Although bees often sting them, honey badgers are not badly affected by the toxin.

Honey badgers sleep in a different hole every night.

HIDING IN HOLES

These animals dig their own holes for sleeping in, or they use holes that have been dug by other animals, such as porcupines. In summer they are nocturnal animals. In cooler weather they sleep at night.

MUST'ELIDS

The mustelid family is a large group of animals that live throughout the world. They are all mammals and carnivores with long bodies and short legs. Most mustelids also have small heads and ears. The largest members of the family are giant otters that grow to more than 5 feet (1.5 m) long.

WOLVERINE

Wolverines deserve their fearsome reputation as ferocious fighters. These mustelids live in the cold north, where animals to hunt are scarce—so any animal they find is potential prey.

A wolverine is strong enough to bring down a bear.

Polecat fur
The fur is mostly dark, but there are pale markings on the face and ears.

BADGERS

Most mustelids live alone, but badgers live in groups called clans. They build tunnels underground that connect to make a large den, called a sett.

A badger lines its tunnels with dried grass and moss.

POLECATS

European polecats live in forests and near water. Their young are called kits, and a female can give birth to as many as ten kits at a time. They hunt at night, searching for mice, rats, voles, frogs, and toads to eat.

Long bodies
Polecats have long bodies and are fast-movers. Like many mustelids, they can run, swim, and climb.

LONG-TAILED WEASEL

Long-tailed weasels hunt rats and mice, which they kill with a quick bite to the neck. Weasels are nocturnal, but they often hunt in the daytime during winter.

Weasels that live in cold places grow white fur in the winter, which helps them hide in snow.

STRONG SMELL

Polecats, like many other mustelids, produce a foul-smelling substance. They release their stink when they are scared, and the smell is so bad that predators—such as foxes—make a fast getaway!

LEOPARD

Leopards are among the world's most successful predators. They are able to survive in many different habitats, from Africa to Asia. These big cats are shy creatures of the night. They rely on silent stealth to catch their prey.

HUNTERS

Leopards are very adaptable cats. They are mostly nocturnal, but they make the most of any opportunity to hunt. They use their keen senses to detect prey.

Tail
A long tail helps a leopard to keep its balance when it jumps or climbs.

PANTHERS

Most leopards have pale fur that is covered with spots, but the colors and spot size can vary.

Some leopards have dark fur and are called black leopards or panthers.

Body
The predator's body stays close to the ground during an attack, so it can move swiftly and silently, without being seen.

FOOD STORE

Like many big cats, leopards do not need to hunt every day. If a leopard kills a large animal it may eat until it is full, then drag the body up into a tree. The leopard will return to eat more when it is hungry again.

Spots
A leopard's markings help to break up its outline, making it harder to see.

The beautiful fur of a snow leopard is long and very thick.

SNOW LEOPARD

Snow leopards live in the cold mountains of Asia where they hunt sheep, hares, and birds. Snow leopards are rare and extremely shy animals, so few people have ever seen one.

Eyes
A leopard's large eyes face forward so it can focus on its prey, and judge how far away it is.

Whiskers
A leopard's whiskers help it to find its way in the dark.

Paws
Large paws are covered in velvet-soft fur to dampen any sound, and huge claws are hidden within.

0   8 ft

SIZE • 3—6¼ FT

FACT FILE

DIET
A range of animals, from small mammals to antelopes

HABITAT
Forests, mountains, grasslands, deserts

BIG CAT'S

Cats are among the most impressive predators of the nocturnal world. With incredibly keen senses, they can find their prey in the dark and overpower them with enormous strength. Their eyes are able to see even in very dim light.

Shock tactics
A female lion grabs a sable antelope by its hind-quarters. Now the antelope cannot use its powerful kick, or its horns, to defend itself.

Tail balance
Most big cats have a large tail that they use to balance while running and leaping.

JAGUARS

Jaguars are big cats of Central and South America. A jaguar's spots are called rosettes, and each has a circle of dark fur.

Jaguars are often found near water, and they are good swimmers.

HUNTING TOGETHER

Most cats hunt alone, but lions live and hunt in groups called prides. Most hunts take place once the sun is setting, when the grasslands become cooler, and other animals graze or visit the waterholes.

SIBERIAN TIGER

The largest big cats are Siberian tigers, but they are extremely rare. These predators hunt in forests or woodlands, where they can hide in the shadows.

LION PREY

Female lions do most of the hunting, and work as a team to locate prey and catch it. They stalk large animals, especially antelopes, buffaloes, and zebras. Groups of lions have even been known to attack elephants.

Siberian tigers are illegally hunted for their coats, and face extinction.

Out in the open
There are few places to hide in the African grasslands, so lions usually hunt out in the open.

Weapons
To catch their prey, top predators such as lions need deadly weapons —teeth and claws—and tremendous speed, agility, and strength.

CARACALS

Caracals are small cats that grow to about 2.5 feet (75 cm) long. They live in Africa and parts of Asia, and they are famous for their pouncing skills—a caracal can jump 10 feet (3 m) in the air.

A caracal, or desert lynx, uses its large ears to listen out for the movements of its prey.

PANGOLIN

There is only one mammal that protects itself with a coat of armor made of special scales: the pangolin, or scaly anteater. There are eight species, or types, of pangolin. They all look similar but they vary in body length from 12 to 70 inches (30–180 cm), not counting their long tails.

CURLED UP

When a pangolin rolls up into a ball, with its large tail wrapped securely around itself, it is protecting its soft belly and head from predators, such as lions, leopards, and hyenas.

When a predator sees a rolled-up pangolin it may prefer to search for prey that is easier to eat.

TOOTHLESS

Unlike most mammals, pangolins do not have teeth. They don't need teeth because they eat tiny ants and termites (ant-like insects), which they gobble up with long sticky tongues and swallow without chewing. A ground pangolin's tongue measures up to 10 inches (25 cm) long—that's about one-third of its body length!

Color
The body is colored brown to olive-green. This color helps the animal to hide among plants.

Tail
The ground pangolin's tail is 16–20 inches (40–50 cm) long. Tree pangolins can use their tails to grip onto branches.

UNDERGROUND

Most pangolins live in Africa. During the day, most of them sleep in burrows that they have dug several feet into the ground. They also use their digging skills to rip apart termite and ant nests, which they find by using their excellent sense of smell.

Long-tailed pangolins have the smallest bodies of any pangolin, but the longest tails.

LONG-TAILED PANGOLIN

Most pangolins live on the ground, but are good climbers and swimmers. Long-tailed pangolins spend most of their time in trees, resting inside hollow trees.

Claws
The pangolin uses its claws to tear open the nests of ants and termites.

Scales
The overlapping scales on a pangolin's body are tough and sharp. There are no scales on its chin, snout, face, and belly.

0   36 in
SIZE • 20–24 IN

FACT FILE

DIET
Insects, especially ants and termites

HABITAT
Grasslands and forests

INSECT-EATERS

Animals that survive on a diet of insects are called insectivores. Insects can make up a nutritious meal, packed with proteins and vitamins, but they are mostly small creatures. This means that they can be tricky to find and catch. It also means that large insectivores have to eat thousands of them every day.

Termite mound
These nests can reach 30 feet (9 m) in height and contain a whole city of termites—a feast for the aardwolf digging its way in.

COLLARED ANTEATER

Anteaters have long snouts, straw-shaped mouths, and long sticky tongues that they use to scoop up ants and termites.

During the day, collared anteaters hide in trees or burrows, and hunt for food in trees during the night.

TERMITE-EATERS

Aardwolves are small cousins of hyenas but, unlike their relatives, these animals only hunt termites and other small insects. They can eat 3,000 termites every night. Aardwolves sleep in dens in the hot African days, and feast in the dark.

WINTER MONTHS

During the winter, there are fewer termites to find, and aardwolves sometimes search for food in the daytime, too. They may lose a lot of weight during the hard winter months, and cubs may struggle to survive.

Grant's golden moles live in sand, and burrow for insects, such as locusts.

Ears
Like many nocturnal animals, aardwolves have large ears so they can listen to the sounds of the night.

GRANT'S GOLDEN MOLE

A Grant's golden mole is about the same size and weight as a mouse. These tiny desert animals are blind, and their noses are covered in leathery skin that keeps sand out of their nostrils.

Body and tail
The body measures up to 30 inches (75 cm) long and the bushy tail is another 12 inches (30 cm). The shoulders are high, and the back slopes toward the tail.

Shoulders
The shoulders are covered in a thick mane, which an aardwolf can raise to make itself look bigger and more menacing.

GREATER BILBY

Bilbies belong to a marsupial family called bandicoots. They dig burrows up to 10 feet (3 m) into the ground.

A greater bilby uses its digging skills to unearth insects hidden in the soil.

VAMPIRE BAT

Vampire bats feed on the blood of other animals—cows and horses especially—but the meal is not very satisfying. They must seek more blood every two days, or they will die of starvation.

FINDING BLOOD

These blood-sucking bats sneak up on their prey at night. They find their victims by sensing their body heat, and then they use the same super-sense to locate blood vessels under the victim's skin.

FALSE VAMPIRES

Asian false vampire bats do not feed on blood. They hunt insects, reptiles, rodents, and even fish instead.

False vampire bats roost in caves, often gathering in groups.

WALKING

These bats crawl, leap, and hop along the ground as they approach their prey. They look clumsy, but they approach with stealth and are rarely noticed by the victim.

EATING AND PEEING

Blood contains a lot of water, so when a vampire bat feeds it urinates (pees) at the same time. If it didn't get rid of the extra water this way, a bat would be too heavy to fly.

Vampire bats use all four limbs to crawl.

0   4 in

SIZE • UP TO 3¾ IN

ON THE ALERT

Vampire bats have excellent senses of smell, sight, and hearing. They use all these senses to locate their prey in the dark. They also listen out for predators such as eagles and hawks.

Like many other bats, vampire bats have large ears for echolocation.

Fur
The body is covered in fine fur.

Teeth
Razor-sharp teeth are used for cutting into a victim's flesh.

Tongue
The tongue has two grooves that help channel blood as it is lapped up.

FACT FILE

DIET
Blood

HABITAT
Caves and tree hollows in warm places

BAT'S

Bats are the only mammals that can fly, rather than glide. Gliding mammals soar on the air, but bats fly using muscle power to flap their wings. Two layers of skin are stretched over the bones of their arms and legs to create the wings. There are two main types of bat: insect-eaters and fruit-eaters.

This fruit bat is licking up the sweet nectar in a flower.

Fingers
The bones in a bat's four fingers are huge, and stretch out to support the membrane of the wing. The thumbs are small and claw-like.

Agile fliers
Bats are agile flyers, and swoop through trees to land on a branch.

FRUIT-EATER
Fruit bats have fox-like faces and large eyes. They rely on their senses of sight and smell to find flowers and ripe fruit. As the bats go from flower to flower, pollen brushes onto their fur, is carried to the next blossom, and pollinates it. Fruit seeds are spat out—or excreted in the bat's droppings—which also helps the plants to spread.

BAT CAVE
Many bats live in large groups called colonies. There are thought to be 20 million free-tailed bats living in one colony in Bracken Cave, Texas.

The sun is setting, and the bats leave their cave to hunt.

Horseshoe bats wrap their wings around themselves when they roost.

JUICE DRINKERS

Fruit bats start feeding as the sun sets, but they often fly about in the day, too. This lesser short-nosed fruit bat likes to suck on soft fruit, drinking the juice and spitting out the pulp.

UPSIDE-DOWN

Bats hang upside-down using claw-like feet that hold on tight even when a bat is asleep—or dead! When they rest, bats are said to be roosting.

Sonar

Fruit bats have heavier bodies than insect-eating bats. The wingspan of a Madagascan flying fox can be more than 50 inches (125 cm).

HUNTING WITH SOUND

Insect-eaters find their food using echolocation. They make sounds called "clicks," and when the sounds hit an insect they bounce back to the bat, which uses information from the echo to work out where the insect is.

AYE-AYE

These animals are so strange that scientists once thought they were bizarre members of the rat family. In fact they are primates— a group that includes monkeys and apes. Aye-ayes are the largest nocturnal primates and they live in Madagascar.

TAPPING

When an aye-aye hunts, it climbs along tree branches, tapping the tree bark as it goes. The aye-aye is listening out for the hollow sound made by a hole in the wood. A hole might be the home of an insect larva—one of this animal's favorite foods.

LONG FINGER

The aye-aye gnaws through the wood to reach a larva. It then uses its long finger to pull out the grub and pop it in its mouth.

An aye-aye's middle finger is long and slender so it can poke into holes.

Ears
The ears are bald and they can move to catch even the smallest sound.

Coat
The fur is coarse, patchy, and tipped in white.

Mouth
The aye-aye's mouth is small, but it contains long incisor teeth that keep growing throughout its life (like a rat's).

The tail is as long as the aye-aye's body and it is very bushy.

LONG TAIL

Aye-ayes are nimble animals. They can run along branches, and leap from tree to tree. Their tails help them to balance.

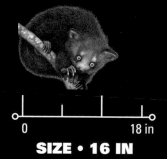

0			18 in

SIZE • 16 IN

⊕ BUILDING NESTS

Nails
Aye-ayes have very long, curved fingernails instead of claws.

Aye-ayes spend most of their time in trees. They build nests from twigs and leaves, where they sleep during the day. Aye-ayes are endangered, which means that they are at risk of becoming extinct.

FACT FILE

DIET
Insect larvae, fruit, seeds, nectar

HABITAT
Rainforest, dry forest

LEMURS

Lemurs are primates that live on the island of Madagascar. Like monkeys and apes, lemurs have big brains, hands, and eyes that face to the front. Lemurs have probably lived in Madagascar for about 60 million years.

RUFFED LEMURS

Many lemurs have bold colors and long tails. Female black-and-white ruffed lemurs line their nests with their own fur.

Black-and-white ruffed lemurs are active during the day and make loud calls to one another.

FAT TAILS

Fat-tailed dwarf lemurs live in forests, where they can make nests in tree-holes. Normally two babies are born at a time. They are looked after by both parents, and they share the nest with older brothers and sisters.

⊕ SLEEPY TIME

Madagascar's winters are cool and dry, with little fruit to eat. To survive, fat-tailed dwarf lemurs become dormant (spend long periods asleep). Before they begin their long rest, they eat a lot of food. It is stored in their tails as fat, to provide the energy they need while they sleep.

Body
The body is about 8 inches (20 cm) long, and the tail is about the same size again.

WESTERN WOOLLY

Nocturnal lemurs, such as woolly lemurs, keep a careful eye out for hawks that hunt at night. The young cling onto their mother's back for the first few months, and stay with her for at least a year.

Fur
The fur is thick and fluffy and there are dark rings around the lemur's large eyes.

Hands
Like other primates, lemurs have hands with thumbs. They can grip tightly onto the branches of a tree as they search for food.

SPORTIVE LEMURS

Sportive lemurs are busy at night, feeding on leaves. As they jump, they twist and turn their bodies so they always land upright, clinging to branches.

Red-tailed sportive lemurs live in the forests of south-western Madagascar.

WOMBAT

Wombats are marsupials that only live in Australia and Tasmania. Like other marsupials, their young are born tiny and are kept in pouches on their mother's belly. Wombats spend most of the daylight hours in burrows, and come out at night to graze.

UNDERGROUND HOMES

There are three different types of wombat. They all dig burrows in grasslands, or in forests of eucalyptus trees. Their burrows can connect to make large underground warrens of many chambers (rooms).

AGGRESSION

Wombats are shy animals, but they can become aggressive toward each other. They kick out with their claws, and bite with sharp teeth.

Hairy-nosed wombats cannot climb but they run fast and are good swimmers.

Nose
Common wombats do not have any hair on the tip of their nose (unlike hairy-nosed wombats).

Head
The head is small and rounded, with small dark eyes and short ears. The jaw muscles are strong, for grinding up plants.

FACT FILE

DIET
Plants, such as grasses and roots

HABITAT
Forests and grassy hills or mountains

Tail
The tail is short, and mostly covered with fur. Wombats have coarse fur that is usually brown with gray tips.

SIZE • 28–47 IN

0   48 in

⊕ BREEDING

Most wombats live in dry places and feed on grass. They only have their young when there has been enough rainfall for plenty of grass to grow. Each mother wombat has one young at a time. A newborn wombat is very small, so it stays in its mother's pouch as it grows, feeding on her milk.

When they are old enough, joeys leave the burrow to graze with their mother.

Legs and claws
Wombats have powerful legs, with broad paws and long claws for digging into soil.

WITH YOUNG OUTSIDE BURROW

Young wombats are called joeys. When they are born, joeys are hairless and blind and just 1 inch (2.5 cm) long. Although they leave the pouch when they are three months old, they return to it to feed and sleep.

MARSUPIALS

Marsupials are a strange group of mammals that mostly live in Australia and its surrounding islands. They include koalas, kangaroos, and wombats. Some marsupials—such as opossums—live in North, Central, and South America. Most marsupials give birth to tiny babies that grow inside a pouch.

DEADLY FOOD?

Koalas spend their lives in eucalyptus trees where they survive on a diet of leaves. The leaves contain a poison but it does not affect koalas because they have special bacteria in their stomachs that destroy the poison.

Legs
The legs are short and the claws are hand-like with long fingers to grip onto branches.

VIRGINIA OPOSSUM

When a Virginia opossum is scared, it rolls over and acts dead, making a foul stink to keep predators away. Virginia opossums live in North America and they eat anything from fruit and eggs to insects and birds.

Virginia opossums climb trees to find food.

EASTERN GRAY KANGAROO

A male gray kangaroo grows to 4½ feet (1.4 m) tall. It can deliver a deadly kick with its powerful legs. These legs cover up to 35 feet (10 m) in one leap.

A female eastern gray kangaroo is carrying a joey in her swollen pouch.

Size
*A koala is about
2½ feet (75 cm) long
and males are larger
than females.*

Head
*Koalas have large
heads with fluffy,
round ears, small eyes,
and large, leathery
nose-pads.*

TASMANIAN DEVIL
Tasmanian devils—or
"tassies"—are ferocious
marsupials that hunt at night,
and also feed on dead
animals. They have a good
sense of smell that helps
them to find food in the dark.

*The jaws of a Tasmanian devil
are huge, and equipped with
large, sharp teeth.*

⊕ KOALA YOUNG
These marsupials can be noisy
animals. At night, the males bellow
and growl to tell other males to stay
away. Joeys stay in their mother's
pouch until they are about six
months old. After that they cling
onto her back.

TREE FROG

Large eyes help many nocturnal animals see in the dark. A red-eyed tree frog's eyes are huge, which not only helps it to see, but also frightens predators away! This amphibian eats insects and catches its prey with a long tongue.

Eyes
During the day, the frog's eyes are shut while it sleeps. If it is disturbed, the eyes pop open, and startle a predator.

Long legs
Tree frogs are good jumpers, but they can also tuck up their legs and sit very still to blend into leaves while stalking their prey.

TOE PADS

A tree frog's foot has large digits (fingers or toes). They are spaced out and tipped with suction pads so they can grip well onto a branch or plant stalk.

Suckers

This is a red-eyed tree frog's front foot, seen from below.

0   3 in

SIZE • 1 ½–2 ¾ IN

Skin
A frog's skin must not dry out.

CROAKING

Red-eyed tree frogs prefer to live close to water. At mating time, males croak loudly, making a "chack-chack" sound, which tells other males to stay away. They also croak to tell females where to find them.

FACT FILE

DIET
Mostly insects, such as crickets and moths

HABITAT
Tropical rainforest

MEMBRANE

A frog has three sets of eyelids. The bottom eyelid does not move. The top eyelid closes when a frog blinks or swallows. The third eyelid is a semi-transparent sheet of skin.

The third eyelid protects the eye when a frog is underwater.

CHANGING COLOR

Most red-eyed tree frogs are brown when they are young and can change color. As they age, they turn bright green with blue sides and orange feet.

LIFE CYCLE

The female lays eggs called spawn, which she glues to a leaf that hangs over a pool of water. The eggs are protected by soft jelly. The young grow inside the eggs. When they hatch, they will fall from the tree into the pool below. The young are called tadpoles, and eventually they will grow legs.

1. Eggs on a leaf

2. Four-day old embryos

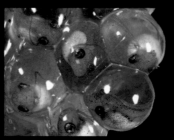

3. Tadpoles

AMPHIBIANS

Amphibians are soft-skinned animals that spend part of their lives in water, and part of their lives on land. When they change their habitat, amphibians go through a process called metamorphosis. There are two main groups of amphibians: frogs and toads, and newts and salamanders.

JAPANESE GIANT SALAMANDER

Most salamanders spend their lives in, or near, water. They have long, slender bodies and a short tail. These amphibians are mostly active at night, and hide during the day.

Japanese giant salamanders grow all their lives, and can be more than 3 feet (1 m) long.

NIGHT MUSIC

Male frogs and toads croak noisily at night to attract a mate. Each species has its own, recognizable call. Many of them puff up a vocal sac (a stretchy membrane on the throat) that makes their calls louder.

SPREADING HABITAT

Cane toads first lived in the Americas, but they now live in Australia and some Pacific Islands, too. They hunt at night and attack almost any animal that is small enough for them to eat. Cane toads have olive-colored skin and grow to 9 inches (23 cm) in length.

BLIND SALAMANDER

Blind salamanders live in caves, where there is little or no light. They probably feed on worms and snails and spend their entire lives underwater.

A blind salamander breathes underwater using these strange, feathery gills.

Lumpy skin
Toads have lumps on their skin, which is often described as "warty."

Glands
There are large glands on either side of the head. These make a milky poison when the toad is scared.

POISON TOAD

Cane toads, their eggs, and their tadpoles all contain a deadly poison. Animals that try to eat them die quickly, and this means that in some areas local wildlife has been badly affected by cane toads.

Legs
Cane toads have short legs that are best suited to crawling. They can make small hops.

GHARIAL

Gharials live in the rivers of northern India. Unlike crocodiles and alligators, gharials do not like coming onto land except to bask in the sun or look after their eggs. They spend most of their lives in water.

Legs
The legs are weak, and the feet are webbed for swimming.

UNDERWATER

When a gharial opens its mouth underwater, a special flap closes its throat to stop water going into its lungs.

Gharials hold their breath because they cannot breathe underwater.

DIGGING A NEST

Females dig holes in a sandy bank when it is time for them to lay their eggs. Each clutch may contain up to 80 eggs. When the baby gharials are ready to hatch, they make little grunting noises so their mother knows it is time to dig them out of their sandy nest.

SIZE • 13–23 FT

0   24 ft

Between 106 and 110 sharp teeth line the snout.

Coloring
Gharials have green-brown bodies, with white underparts.

Smooth scales
Gharials have smooth scales on their body, unlike crocodiles and alligators, which have rough scales.

LONG SNOUT
As a gharial hunts underwater, it swipes its jaws from side to side. The teeth of a gharial are perfectly shaped for grabbing onto slippery fish.

Long and slender
The snout is very long and slender, and males have a swollen tip on the end of it. A gharial's snout grows longer and thinner as it gets older.

⊕ SENSITIVE SKIN
Special places in a gharial's skin help it feel the movement of other animals nearby, which means it can find fish even at night. Gharials keep very still underwater, lying in wait for a fish to swim by, before snatching it whole. However, they must have their heads above water before they gulp the fish down.

FACT FILE

DIET
Fish

HABITAT
Quiet parts of fast-flowing rivers

CROCODILES

Many nocturnal animals like to spend the daylight hours hiding from predators, but members of the crocodilian family are afraid of nothing. They lie in the hot sun, soaking up the heat, and wait until sunset before they go hunting.

Stealth
An alligator can keep most of its body hidden underwater while it moves silently and stealthily closer to its prey.

CAIMAN EYE
Crocodiles have a transparent third eyelid that covers the eye when the animal is underwater. Scientists think they can see shadows and shapes even when this eyelid is closed.

*A **caiman's eye** is large, to help it see in the dark.*

LEAPING
Some crocodiles and alligators leap out of water to grab prey. They are not choosy, and will attack almost any animal they can find. These predators have hardly changed in 200 million years and are sometimes called "living fossils."

Nile crocodiles often come ashore to warm their bodies on hot days.

DEADLY SPIN

Nile crocodiles are strong enough to pull large animals, such as buffaloes, into the water. They cannot chew, so they spin around underwater with their prey in their jaws, ripping and breaking it up into bite-sized pieces.

Eyes and nostrils
The eyes and nostrils are positioned on the top of the head, so the reptile can still see, smell, and breathe.

ALLIGATOR TYPES

There are only two types of alligator: American and Chinese. American alligators are huge and heavy reptiles, while Chinese alligators are much smaller, and extremely rare.

This is the skull of a Nile crocodile.

SKULL
Crocodilians have large, sharp teeth. When a crocodile's mouth is closed, two teeth on their lower jaws are still visible. When an alligator's mouth is closed, no teeth can be seen.

BARN OWL

Barn owls are also known as screech or demon owls because they do not hoot. Instead, they make a scary scream as they fly through the night sky—although sometimes they hiss, or they even make a snoring sound!

HOVERING

When hovering above its prey, the owl spreads its wings and fans its tail feathers.

The bird must focus on the prey before it makes the final plunge.

Talons
An owl's claws are called talons. They are long and pointed—the perfect shape for grabbing a small animal as it tries to escape.

RESTING

These large birds spend most of the day resting in holes in trees, or in places such as barns. Like most owls, barn owls prefer woodland and forest habitats, or grasslands where there are small mammals to hunt.

NIGHT-HUNTER

Barn owls mostly hunt at night, but if they have chicks to feed, they may start searching for food in the daytime, too. The eyes of a barn owl are large and face forward. This gives the owl superb night vision. It can see far distances, and it can focus on small prey, such as a mouse. It also has superb hearing.

Large eyes mean that owls can see much better than us in the dark.

TUBE-SHAPED EYES

An owl's eyeballs are tube-shaped, not round. An owl cannot move its eyes, so when it wants to see something to the side, it must move its whole head.

Plumage
A barn owl's plumage (feathering) is mostly white and golden.

Face
The face is heart-shaped, and collects the slightest sound.

Feathers
An owl's feathers are soft, with fluffy edges. This helps to muffle the sound an owl makes as it flies.

0   18 in

SIZE • 11½–17½ IN

FACT FILE

DIET
Small mammals

HABITAT
Everywhere except deserts and polar places

OWLS

Owls are large birds of prey that hunt at night. Like other raptors (birds of prey), owls have long talons and sharp beaks. Owls live all over the world, except in Antarctica. Although they are common in many places, few people ever see them in action.

LONG, COLD NIGHTS

In the Arctic, the winter nights are long and cold and snowy owls begin to hunt as soon as the sun goes down. In the summer, the day lasts almost 24 hours and snowy owls must search for prey in daylight instead.

Camouflage
A female has black marks on her white plumage. This helps her to hide among rocks when she is nesting on the ground.

FISHING OWL

Most owls hunt little mammals, such as mice, but fishing owls scoop their slippery prey straight out of the water.

Fishing owls have extra-long, sharp talons for grabbing on to fish.

HUNTING IN THE SNOW

Snowy owls soar over the Arctic landscape, looking for small animals such as rabbits and lemmings to eat. They have such superb senses of sight and hearing that they can even find animals that are covered in snow.

Huge wingspan
A snowy owl's wingspan— the distance from wingtip to wingtip—is enormous at up 5 feet (150 cm).

Burrowing owls have a piercing stare and yellow eyes.

BURROWING OWL
Little burrowing owls are unusual birds that make their nests underground. They sometimes dig their own holes, but they usually take over holes that were made by other animals.

LONG-EARED OWL
Long-eared owls mostly rely on their sense of hearing to find their prey. They can even catch mice in complete darkness.

These owls have ear tufts. Their multicolored feathers help them hide in woodland.

Sharp claws
The owl's talons are covered in fluffy feathers to keep its feet warm in Arctic snow and ice.

COMMON GLOW WORM

Wingless
Female glow worms do not have wings.

The common glow worm lives in forests, meadows, and marshes throughout Europe and Asia. Both males and females glow to attract a mate, although the male shines much less brightly. The female stops producing light once she has mated. She will then lay her eggson or just below the ground surface.

LOOKING FOR LOVE

Only the male glow worm has wings. He flies around until he spots a glowing female.

The male glow worm is a little over half the size of the female.

Wingless
Female glow worms do not have wings.

Light organs
The glowing light is made by chemical reactions inside the body.

MASS DISPLAY

In Southeast Asia, thousands of glow worms, or fireflies, gather in trees, flashing their lights on and off together to attract mates. They can use a variety of steady glows and flashes to communicate during this courtship ritual.

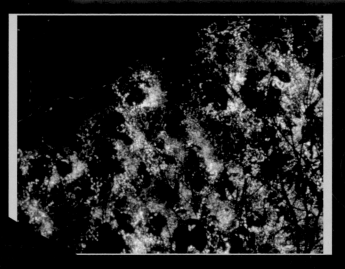

Antenna
Glow worms smell by using their antennae.

Mouth parts
Adult glow worms do not eat. They die after mating.

Leg
The females climb up grass stems or twigs to display their glowing tails.

⊕ ATTRACTING ATTENTION

The female common glow worm cannot fly. At night, she waves her glowing tail at the sky to attract passing males. The males can see the light from more than 150 feet (50 m) away. This light can be yellow, green, or pale red in color.

FEMALE • 4/5 IN

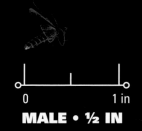

MALE • 1/2 IN

FACT FILE

DIET
Larvae hunt slugs and snails on the forest floor

HABITAT
Grasslands and woodlands

FIREFLIES

Also known as lightning bugs or glow worms, fireflies are actually beetles. Their name comes from the bright, yellow-green light produced by their bodies. On summer nights, they can often be seen lighting up trees and shining out from the undergrowth. Some 2,000 species live in tropical and temperate parts of the world.

LARVAL KILLERS

The larvae of most firefly species are predators, feeding on insects, snails, and even other larvae. Some adults also hunt, while others eat nectar.

This firefly larva is feeding on the body of a snail.

LIGHT IN THE DARK

Fireflies flash their lights in the darkness to attract mates. Each species has its own pattern of flashes—a kind of "signal" that allow fireflies of the same species to recognize one another.

Body
The light is produced by organs in the firefly's abdomen.

Female firefly
Females are much bigger than the males.

Antenna

Wings

COME ON OVER

In some species, it is the male who flashes to attract the female, while in others, the females do the "calling." Fireflies use different lengths of flashes, long and short, and can also change the frequency and brightness of their signals.

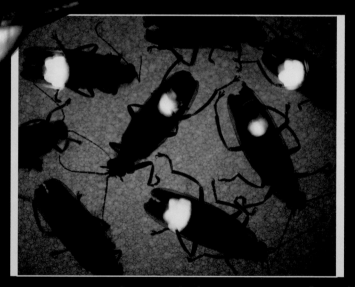

KEEP OFF

Some fireflies also use their lights in self-defense. The flashes can distract or frighten a predator, while in some species the lights warn their enemies they have a nasty taste.

LIFE CYCLE

Eggs hatch five weeks after laying. The larvae crawl out and spend up to a year feeding and growing before pupating and then turning into adults.

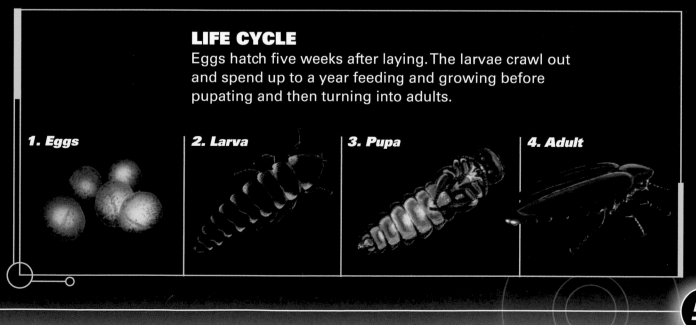

1. Eggs   **2. Larva**   **3. Pupa**   **4. Adult**

RAILROAD WORM

Railroad worms are beetles, not worms, but when they are young, they look like worms or maggots and they are able to glow in the dark. Found in North and South America, they survive by biting the heads off millipedes and sucking out the liquid from inside them!

Body
The 11 hairy segments, or parts, each have three spots that glow with a greenish-yellow color. The spots of light are called lanterns.

ADULTS

Even when the female railroad worms become adults, they still look like the young, or larvae. The males, however, are long, slender beetles with wings, six legs, large eyes, and long antennae (feelers).

Head
There are two lanterns on the female's head, which glow red.

BIOLUMINESCENCE

Animals that make their own light are described as bioluminescent. The colors on a railroad worm are made when special chemicals mix together in their bodies.

The lanterns on the side of the insect's body may scare predators away.

Jaws
Two grooved mandibles for biting and extracting liquids

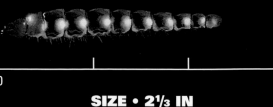

ACTUAL SIZE

0   3 in

SIZE • 2¹/₃ IN

A female larva (below) alongside a male railroad worm larva.

LARVAE
Young beetles are called larvae. Male railroad worm larvae are much smaller than females. They will both change into adults, but the females will still look like larvae.

Legs
The six legs each have one claw, which grip the ground as the animal crawls and burrows.

PROTECTING EGGS
Adult females lay about 12 hard, round eggs and then wrap themselves around the eggs for the first few days.

The eggs develop into larvae, which will start to glow as soon as they hatch.

⊕ ROWS OF LIGHTS
Seen from the side, the lights on a railroad worm's body are arranged in three long rows of light, making it look a little like a train in the dark. That's why it is called the railroad worm, or the night train. It is thought that the railroad worm's head lanterns shine light on prey, while the lanterns on the side of its body scare predators away.

FACT FILE

DIET
Millipedes

HABITAT
Farmland, grasslands and woods

BEETLES

There are about 400,000 types of beetle, and they make up one-third of all insects. They have six legs and a pair of soft wings for flying. They are protected by a special pair of hard wings called elytra. Most beetles eat plants, but some of them are night-time hunters.

Giant beetles
Male Hercules beetles can grow to 7 inches (17 cm) long, including their horns. The females are smaller.

LIFE CYCLE

Female Hercules beetles lay their eggs in the rotting trunks of trees. After one month, the eggs hatch and a large maggot, or larva, emerges from each one. The maggots eat and grow for up to 18 months, and male maggots can grow to 6 inches (15 cm) long.

Hard wing cases
This beetle can unfold the flight wings under its elytra to fly a short distance.

CHRISTMAS BEETLE
There are about 35 different types of Christmas beetle. They are named after the time of year when they are most common.

Adult Christmas beetles climb trees to reach the leaves they eat.

FOREST DWELLERS

Hercules beetles live in forests in Central and South America. They are active at night, feeding on fruit and the liquid sap found inside trees and plants, especially palms.

Cockchafers have hairy bodies and feathery feelers.

COCKCHAFER

Nocturnal beetles are in danger from night-time predators such as owls and bats. Cockchafers, for example, fly between trees, feeding on leaves. The adults only live for one month, but many are eaten before then.

Strong horns
Males have large horns that grow out of their heads. They are very strong and can use their horns to lift weights of up to 5 pounds (2 kg)!

DARKLING BEETLE

Most darkling beetles have black elytra and they feed on living or rotting plants. They feed at night to avoid being seen by the birds, reptiles, and rodents that eat them.

Legs
There are three pairs of legs that each end in a pair of claws for gripping surfaces as the beetle clambers about.

A scared darkling beetle stands tall and makes a foul stink to scare predators away.

FUNGUS GNAT

Little fungus gnats thrive in warm, damp places. Most types of fungus gnat live in forests but some of them (in New Zealand and Australia) spend part of their lives in caves, where there is no natural light. The young of these fungus gnats are called glowworms.

Silk threads
The larva spins extra threads of silk to form a protective barrier around its tubular nest of transparent mucus.

HANGING

The larvae spin silk, which they use to make traps that hang from a cave ceiling, or from trees in the forest. The larvae produce a light in their tails, which they wave to attract flying insects toward the traps.

Tail light
The light from the larva's tail make its silky threads sparkle.

CAUGHT PREY

Small insects, such as midges, are attracted by the glowworms and fly into the silken snares, where they become trapped. The glowworm pulls the silken thread up so it can grab the prey and eat it.

A trapped fly cannot escape the sticky, toxic silk.

Growing up
The larva spends up to one year feeding from a cave ceiling before turning into a pupa.

The hanging silken threads are called "snares."

HANGING TRAPS

Some types of fungus gnat place drops of a toxic liquid on the hanging curtains of silk threads. There can be hundreds or thousands of snares hanging in a single cave.

Closing in
The larva emerges from the tube when a struggling prey makes the threads vibrate.

Sticky traps
Long silken threads are coated with droplets of sticky mucus. Each strand of thread is about 16 inches (40 cm) long.

⊕ FOREVER YOUNG?

Most fungus gnats live in a permanently dark habitat where they mainly feed on fungus. These cave-dwellers spend most of their lives as larvae that eat and grow, increasing their size ten times before they change into adults. These hardy insects can survive freezing temperatures.

FACT FILE

DIET
Flying insects

HABITAT
Caves or damp, dark forests

LIVING IN CAVES

Some cave-dwelling animals escape into the light from time to time, while others live in eternal darkness. Without sunlight, they have adapted over time to one of the planet's strangest habitats. Many cave-dwellers are either blind or have poor eyesight.

BLIND FISH

Blind cavefish live in warm, dark caves in Mexico, and are also known as Mexican tetras. There is another kind of Mexican tetra that lives in pools and rivers above ground, and is able to see. Tetras feed mainly on small crustaceans, insects, and worms.

Body
The body grows up to 5 inches (12 cm) long.

Eyeless
Cavefish are born with eyes, but as they grow older, skin covers them.

CAVE CRICKET

Cave crickets live in dark places, including caves, basements, and garages. They are either blind, or can only see a small amount of light.

Cave crickets have very long antennae (feelers).

HUNTING IN THE DARK

Blind tetras have either blind eyes, or no eyes at all. But they have sharp teeth and they are good hunters, using their other senses of taste, smell, and touch to find small prey. They also scavenge on the remains of dead animals in the water.

This is a cave crayfish from Florida.

CAVE CRAYFISH
Cave crayfish are blind, but they have good senses of smell and touch. They have no color in their shell-like skin and are mostly smaller than 2 inches (5 cm) long.

Transparent scales
The tail, fins, and body are covered in scales that are mostly colorless, revealing the pinkish skin underneath.

Lateral line
This is a sensitive area that all fish possess. Using its lateral line, a blind cavefish can sense movement in the water to find its way around and detect prey.

CAVE BEETLE
Most ground beetles are nocturnal, but some live in caves, in permanent darkness. Some types of blind cave beetles are extremely rare, and are only found in one cave.

Blind cave beetles find their way using sensitive feelers called antennae.

UNDERWING MOTH

Underwing moths spend the daylight hours resting on a tree trunk, where the mottled colors of their forewings are perfectly camouflaged against brown and gray bark.

BOLD COLORS

There are many different types of underwing moths, and the bold colors of their hind wings vary from blue to dull pink and bright red.

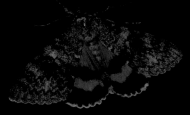

The bold hind wings, or "underwings," give this group of moths its name.

⊕ GREAT HEARING

Like many other nocturnal moths, underwings have excellent hearing. As they fly at night, they listen out for bats, which feed on them. This sweetheart underwing moth lives in eastern North America.

HUNGRY CATERPILLAR

Caterpillars are also known as larvae. They are the young of moths and butterflies and they often feed at night.

Underwing caterpillars grow plump before preparing to change into adult moths.

⊕ LAYING EGGS

Adults lay their eggs in late summer, near the plants the caterpillars will eat, or within tree bark cracks. After they hatch in spring, the sweetheart underwing caterpillars mostly feed on two types of plant: cottonwood and willow.

Forewings
The forewings have gray edges on the upper side. The dull patterns provide good camouflage on tree bark.

FACT FILE

DIET
Nectar

HABITAT
Grasslands, forests and near water

Sense organs
Moths have large eyes and sensitive antennae (feelers).

Legs
Like all other insects, moths have three pairs of legs.

Hindwings
Seen here from underneath, the hind wings have bold stripes that are brightest on the upper side of the wing.

DEFENSE
The underwing moth's bright colors resemble the eyes of a predator such as a cat, and may scare potential attackers. The moth flashes open its wings if disturbed.

Opening the forewings reveals a flash of color that will startle a predator.

MOTHS

There is no real difference between moths and butterflies, but in general moths tend to feed at night and butterflies are more active in the daytime. Moths are more often dull-colored, and have larger antennae. Both moths and butterflies are superb fliers, flitting from plant to plant, and both can uncurl a straw-shaped proboscis to sip nectar and other liquids.

Feathery feelers
The moth's two antennae are long and comb-like. Males have larger antennae than females.

Two pairs of wings
The Spanish moon moth has a wingspan of 2¾–4 inches (7–10 cm).

HAWK MOTHS
Hawk moths are among the fastest flying insects, topping 12 miles per hour (20 kph). Some can even hover like a hummingbird while sipping nectar from each flower.

With pink and green markings, the elephant hawk moth is easy to recognize when it appears at dusk.

SENSITIVE SMELL
Moth antennae are feathery or comb-like. As nocturnal creatures, moths benefit from having antennae that are very sensitive to smell.

Male moths have bigger antennae so they can find females by their smell.

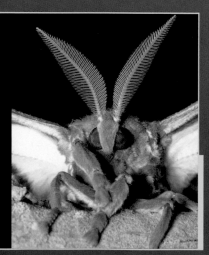

⊕ TAILED MOTHS

Spanish moon moths belong to the Saturnid family of moths, which includes the largest and some of the most beautiful of all moths. Their hind wings have long "tails," and the scales on the wings have a green metallic sheen.

Eye spots
Spanish moon moths have an eye spot on the wings to confuse predators.

A puss moth's strange appearance scares other animals away.

PUSS MOTHS

Adult puss moths have fluffy, creamy-white bodies. Their caterpillars, however, are colorful. They have fake eyes and hind legs that are long and whip-like.

⊕ SPANISH MOON MOTH

These spectacular moths live in the pine forests of France and Spain. Females lay a brood of about 100 eggs, which hatch into caterpillars that feed on pine needles. The adults do not eat and survive only a few days while they find a mate and lay their eggs.

GIANT DESERT HAIRY SCORPION

Although scorpions belong to the same family of animals as spiders, they look and behave very differently. Most scorpions live in dry places and they do not make silk.

Tail
The long tail is made up of segments and bends over the animal's body, ready to strike.

STING
The tail has five regular segments, and the sixth contains venom glands and the sharp stinger.

⊕ STING IN THE TAIL
Scorpions are equipped with a venomous sting, which is delivered by the animal's long, slender tail. The stings are used on prey, but scorpions also use them to defend themselves. Giant desert hairy scorpions often run from danger, and hide in burrows.

ULTRAVIOLET GLOW
Strangely, scorpions glow when ultraviolet light is shone on them. No one knows why.

Grasping prey
Scorpions use their powerful claws to grab prey before stinging it.

It is easy for scientists to track glow-in-the-dark scorpions.

FACT FILE

DIET
Insects, lizards, scorpions, small mammals

HABITAT
Rocky deserts and scrubland

Exoskeleton
The scorpion's body is protected by a hard exoskeleton.

Legs
There are four pairs of walking legs.

ARACHNIDS

Arachnids have roamed the planet for at least 400 million years. They are such a successful group of animals that there are more than 100,000 different types, ranging from little mites to spiders the size of dinner plates. Most arachnids are predators and live on land.

Body parts
Like all arachnids, whip scorpions have two main body parts and four pairs of legs.

Powerful claws
Two claws—the pedipalps—are big and strong. Whip scorpions use their pedipalps for burrowing and crushing prey.

HARVESTMAN
Harvestmen are sometimes called daddy-long-legs. They have small bodies, and a legspan that can reach 4 inches (10 cm) across.

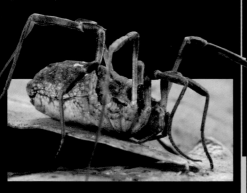

A harvestman looks like a spider, but it has a rounded body without a waist.

WHIP SCORPIONS
Whip scorpions are also called vinegaroons because they can spray vinegar-like acid over other animals. Whip scorpions have a good aim. They can hit an attacker more than 20 inches (50 cm) away.

Extra-long legs
The front two legs are very long, and they are used like feelers.

⊕ ON THE HUNT

When a whip scorpion is hunting, it uses its long front legs to feel its way in the dark. Once it has found a victim, the whip-scorpion grabs and crushes it with its massive pedipalps.

Whip-like tail
The whip-like tail can be as long as the scorpion's entire body. It does not have a sting.

Young scorpions are protected by their mother.

Acid holes
A whip scorpion sprays acid from holes in its body.

MOTHER CARRYING YOUNG

Although most arachnids do not take care of their young, scorpions are good mothers. They carry their brood on their back until the babies have molted once.

PSEUDOSCORPION

False scorpions have a similar shape to scorpions but they do not have tails and stingers. Like spiders, they have venomous bites. They also make silk, which they use to build nests.

This European false scorpion is just 0.1 inch (3 mm) long.

WOLF SPIDER

Many spiders trap their prey in webs, but wolf spiders chase and ambush their prey instead. These large spiders run and jump, and spend most of their lives on the ground.

CAMOUFLAGED HUNTERS

Most wolf spiders are colored dull brown or gray so that they are camouflaged on the ground. They hunt insects or other spiders, especially among leaf litter on a forest floor.

CLOSE UP
The largest two eyes are probably used for seeing an image while the smaller eyes may be of more use in sensing movement.

Wolf spiders need good eyesight to hunt fast-moving prey.

0   1½ in

SIZE • UP TO 1½ IN

Legs
All spiders have eight legs that have many joints and are covered in tiny hairs. The legs can taste, smell, and sense movement.

THREAT POSE

Spiders are not very sociable animals and they usually live alone. If two male spiders bump into each other, they may threaten each other, or even fight.

Eyes
Most spiders, including wolf spiders, have eight eyes that are arranged in three rows.

A male Russian wolf spider raises its legs to ward other spiders away.

Fangs
The chelicerae are grabbing mouthparts with fangs. The fangs are curved and sharp and connected to venom glands.

FACT FILE

DIET
Invertebrates, especially insects or spiders

HABITAT
Almost anywhere on land

A tarantula wolf spider hides in its burrow.

BURROW

Some wolf spiders make themselves burrows, which they line in silk. From this place of safety, they can launch an attack on a passing bug.

SPIDERS

All spiders have eight legs and can spin sticky silk threads from the back of their bodies. Their bodies are divided into two main parts—the head and the abdomen (unlike insects, which have three main body parts). Most spiders live on land and are nocturnal hunters. They belong to a group of animals called arachnids, which includes scorpions and ticks.

KING BABOON SPIDER

A king baboon spider can grow to 8 inches (20 cm) long. When it is scared it raises itself up on its hindlegs, waves its front legs, and shows off its huge fangs.

Hidden hunter
Goldenrod crab spiders are often found on pale flowers, and are able to change their color so they are perfectly camouflaged.

Grabbing prey
Crab spiders grab their prey with the front two pairs of legs, which are longer and thinner than the other legs.

⊕ SIDE WALKING

Crab spiders tend to move sideways like crabs, which is how they got their name. They ambush insects that visit the flowers to feed on the nectar, and have venom that is strong enough to kill insects much larger than themselves.

TARANTULA

A Mexican red-kneed tarantula grows to 6 inches (15 cm) long and females can live for 25 years or more. Its fangs inject its victims with venom.

Tarantulas can kill large prey, including reptiles , birds, and small mammals.

⊕ SUCKING FOOD

Crab spiders feed by first vomiting onto their victim. The fluid they vomit turns part of the victim to liquid, which the spider sucks up.

WANDERER

Brazilian wandering spiders have huge venom glands and each spider has enough venom to kill more than 200 mice.

It takes just seconds for the venom of a wandering spider to kill a katydid.

GLOSSARY

AMPHIBIAN
A cold-blooded animal with soft skin that can live on land and in water. An amphibian usually lays its eggs in water. Frogs and toads are amphibians.

ANTENNAE
A pair of thin appendages on the heads of arthropods and some sea animals. Antennae are used for smelling, tasting, and feeling.

ARACHNID
Invertebrate animals with eight legs. Spiders, scorpions, amd harvestmen are arachnids. Almost all arachnids live on land.

ARTHROPOD
An animal with an exoskeleton and jointed legs. Arthropods do not have backbones. Insects, spiders, and scorpions are all arthropods.

BIOLUMINESCENCE
The making of light by a living organism. Fire flies, glow worms, and many deep-sea creatures generate light using chemicals in their bodies.

CAMOUFLAGE
Body colors and patterns that make an animal blend in with its surroundings.

CANID
The family of carnivores that includes dogs, wolves, foxes, jackals, and coyotes.

CARAPACE
The tough upper section of the exoskeleton found on spiders, scorpions, and other arachnids.

CARNIVORE
An animal that eats only meat.

CHELICERAE
The mouthparts of arthropods. In most spiders, chelicerae contain venom glands and are used to inject venom into prey.

DIURNAL
An animal is diurnal if it is active during the day.

DORMANCY
A sleep-like state in which an animal stops being active, for example in winter.

ECHOLOCATION
A way in which animals such as bats navigate, avoid obstacles, or locate prey in the dark by sending out high-pitched bursts of sound and detecting the echo, or reflections.

ELYTRA
The hardened forewings found in certain insects, such as beetles. They protect the hind wings, which are usually transparent.

ENDANGERED ANIMAL
A species of animal that is in danger of dying out completely, or becoming extinct.

EXOSKELETON
A skeleton forming a hard shell around the outside of a body, such as an insect's.

INSECTIVORE
An animal that eats only insects.

INVERTEBRATE

An animal that does not have a backbone. Most animals are invertebrates. Some have a hard outer exoskeleton, while others have soft bodies.

LARVAE

The young of animals such as fish, insects, and amphibians. The larvae often look completely different from the adults.

LIVING FOSSIL

An organism that closely resembles its ancient fossilized ancestors. Crocodiles and alligators are examples of living fossils.

MAMMAL

A warm-blooded animal that feeds its young with milk. Mammals are usually covered with hair or fur. Most mammals give birth to live young.

MARSUPIAL

A type of mammal whose young finish developing in their mother's pouch, not inside the womb.

MUSTELID

A family of carnivorous mammals that includes badgers, weavers, otters, and wolverines.

NOCTURNAL

An animal is nocturnal if it is active at night.

PEDIPALP

A small, leg-like appendage on either side of a spider's mouth, used for tasting and smelling.

PREHENSILE

Able to curl around things and grip them tightly. Pit vipers and pangolins have prehensile tails.

PROBOSCIS

A long, nose-like set of mouthparts. The long tongue of moths and butterflies is a proboscis.

PUPA

An insect that develops inside a cocoon, between its larval and adult stages.

RAPTOR

A bird of prey that hunts and feeds on other animals. Eagles and owls are examples of raptors.

REPTILE

A group of animals that have scaly skin and lay eggs. Reptiles are cold-blooded, which means they cannot keep their body temperature constant. Crocodiles, turtles, and lizards are all reptiles.

SCALES

Small protective plates that form part of the outer skin of some animals. Fish have bony scales, while reptiles and birds have scales made of keratin (a hard fiber made of protein).

SPAWN

Eggs of animals that live in water, such as fish and frogs.

VENOM

A toxic (poisonous) substance used by animals such as snakes and spiders to paralyze or kill prey. Some animals possess venom as a form of self-defense. For example, the cane toad's skin is highly toxic to most animals.

VERTEBRATE

An animal that has a backbone. Fish, amphibians, reptiles, birds, and mammals are vertebrates.

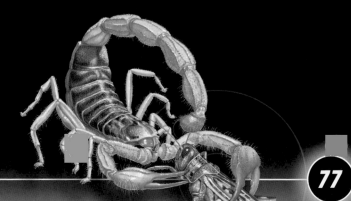

INDEX

ACKNOWLEDGMENT'S

Picture credits

(t=top, b=bottom, l=left, r=right, c=center, fc=front cover)

ALAMY: ©PhotoAlto/Alamy 64 tcl, ©Andrew Darrington/Alamy 64 br,

FLPA: Thomas Marent/Minden Pictures/FLPA 6 bl, 6-7 c, Jelger Herder 6 tc, Buiten-beeld/Minden Pictures/FLPA 7 tc, Terry Whittaker/FLPA 7 tr, 10 l, Michael Quinton/Minden Pictures/FLPA 8 bl, Fabrice Simon/Biosphoto/FLPA 8-9 c, Tim Fitzharris/ Minden Pictures/FLPA 9 r, Tui De Roy/Minden Pictures/FLPA 10-11 c, Cecile Bloch/Biosphoto/FLPA 11 tr, Dickie Duckett/FLPA 11 br, Konrad Wothe/Minden Pictures/FLPA 12 l, Frans Lanting/FLPA 14 cl, 23 br, 25 tr, 26 bl, 32 bl, 42 c, Yossi Eshbol/FLPA 13 tr, David Hosking/FLPA 13 cr, 18 bl, 24 cl, Winfried Wisniewski/FLPA 14 tr, Matthias Breiter/Minden Pictures/FLPA 14-15 c, 18 cr, 23 tr, Chris & Tilde Stuart/FLPA 15 tr, 16 bl, Marcel Langelaan/Minden Pictures/FLPA 15 br, Philip Perry/FLPA 17 br, Michael Quinton/ Minden Pictures/FLPA 19 br, Gerard Lacz/FLPA 20 bl, Thomas Marent/Minden Pictures/FLPA 21 tr, F1online/F1online/FLPA 22 bl, Pete Oxford/Minden Pictures/FLPA 22-23 c, Dave Watts/Biosphoto/FLPA 26-27 c, 37 br, Michael & Patricia Fogden/Minden Pictures/FLPA 27 tr, 29 tr, 41 br, 51 tr, 61 tr, 66 bcl, Eric Woods/FLPA 27 br, Frank W Lane/FLPA 28 tcl, Chien Lee/Minden Pictures/ 29 tr, 30 bl, Kevin Schafer/Minden Pictures/FLPA 30 bc, Konrad Wothe/Minden Pictures/FLPA 30-31 c, 33 tr, Sylvain Cordier/ Biosphoto/FLPA 31 tr, Paul van Hoof, Buiten-beeld/Minden Pictures/FLPA 34 bl, Nicolas Cegalerba/Biosphoto/FLPA 34-35 c, 35 br, 42 bl, Albert Visage/FLPA 35 tr, Jurgen & Christine Sohns/FLPA 36 bl, Yva Momatiuk & John Eastcott/Minden Pictures/FLPA 38 bl, S & D & K Maslowski/FLPA 38 cl, Suzi Eszterhas/Minden Pictures/FLPA 38-39 c, John Holmes/FLPA 39 tr, Ingo Arndt/ Minden Pictures/FLPA 40 bl, 40 tcr, 70 cr, Peter Wilson/FLPA 40 br, Christian Ziegler/Minden Pictures/FLPA 41 bc, Photo Researchers/FLPA 42 cl, 43 tr, 46 bl, 63 tr, 70-71 c, 75 br, ZSSD/Minden Pictures/FLPA 44 bl, Mark Newman/FLPA 45 tr, IMAGEBROKER, CHRISTIAN HÃ¼TTER/Imagebroker/FLPA 46-47 c, ImageBroker/Imagebroker/FLPA 47 tcr, Chris & Tilde Stuart/ FLPA 47 bcr, Jules Cox/FLPA 48 cl, Jelger Herder/Minden Pictures/FLPA 49 tr, Claude Balcaen/Biosphoto/FLPA 50 bl, Chris van Rijswijk/Minden Pictures/FLPA 50-51 c, Mark Schuurman/Minden Pictures/FLPA 51 br, Mitsuhiko Imamori/Minden Pictures/FLPA 53 tr, 58-59 c, Chris Mattison/FLPA 58 bl, IMAGEBROKER, MARCUS SIEBERT/Imagebroker/FLPA 59 tr, Mark Moffett/Minden Pictures/FLPA 59 br, 66 bcl, Emanuele Biggi/FLPA 62 bl, 63 br, 72 bl, 73 tr, 74 tcl, Gerard Lacz/FLPA 62-63 c, Kevin Elsby/FLPA 66 bl, Thomas Marent/Minden Pictures/FLPA 66-67 c, 67 cr, Erica Olsen/FLPA 68 cl, Albert Lleal/Minden Pictures/FLPA 68 bl, Dave Pressland/FLPA 70 bl, 74-75 c, D Jones/FLPA 71 br, Philip Bildstein/Imagebroker/FLPA 73 br, Chris Shields/Minden Pictures/FLPA 75 tr

Getty: National Geographic/Getty Images 56 bl, 57 tr, 60 bl,

Naturepl: Nature Production/naturepl 54 bl, Visuals Unlimited/naturepl 55 cr

Shutterstock: Christian Musat 17 cr, BMJ 18-19 c viphotos 70-71 c

Superstock: Animals Animals 28 bl, Ann and Steve Toon / Robert Harding picture library 48-49c

WIKI: Creative Commons Attribution 3.0 Unported 64 bl